WOMEN DAREDEVILS

Thrills, Chills, AND *Frills*

Julie Cummins

illustrated by

Cheryl Harness

PUFFIN BOOKS

To Blair, who always dares me to take one more step
J.C.

For the daring Ms. Kit
C.H.

PUFFIN BOOKS
An imprint of Penguin Random House LLC
375 Hudson Street
New York, New York 10014

First published in the United States of America by Dutton Children's Books,
a division of Penguin Young Readers Group, 2008
Published by Puffin Books, an imprint of Penguin Random House LLC, 2015

Text copyright © 2008 by Julie Cummins
Illustrations copyright © 2008 by Cheryl Harness

THE LIBRARY OF CONGRESS HAS CATALOGED THE DUTTON CHILDREN'S BOOKS EDITION AS FOLLOWS:
Cummins, Julie.
Women daredevils: thrills, chills, and frills / by Julie Cummins; illustrated by Cheryl Harness.
p. cm.
ISBN: 978-0-525-47948-2 (hardcover)
I. Women daredevils—Biography—Juvenile literature. I. Harness, Cheryl, ill. II. Title.
GV1839.C86 2008
791.'0922—dc22 [B] 2007018102

Puffin Books ISBN 978-0-14-751737-1

Manufactured in China

1 3 5 7 9 10 8 6 4 2

CONTENTS

INTRODUCTION

If you think you've seen every kind of "extreme sport" on television, hold onto your chinstrap and wait until you read about these fourteen amazing daredevils. They were individuals who endangered their lives performing death-defying stunts to entertain the public. They defied gravity, flew without wings, plunged into watery depths, *and* they were WOMEN!

The term *daredevil* conjures up scary scenes of motorcycle riders, high-wire artists, supersonic pilots, or skyscraper climbers. A daredevil's act is that breath-holding, heart-stopping moment when we know that one misstep could end in a terrible accident or even death. It leaves us amazed, awestruck, and astonished, with our mouths hanging open.

Our fascination with outlandish sports is not new. At the turn of the century, the demands of everyday life left little opportunity for amusement; there were no movies, television, or Internet, which made live performances by daredevils the primary entertainment of the times. People would travel on horseback, by boat, on trains, or in wagons to be entertained by live "reality shows."

The chill of the thrill never loses it appeal. In the 1920s, world-renowned magician Harry Houdini performed death-defying underwater escapes. In the 1970s, stunt biker Evel Knievel set a world record by jumping his motorcycle across nineteen Dodge cars. Today, twenty-first-century magician and mystifier David Blaine flabbergasts people with his extreme stunts of endurance: being buried alive inside a glass coffin and frozen in time inside a closet of ice. These men have risked their lives and held men, women, and children spellbound.

Like these three daring headliners, most of the audacious stunt performers at the turn of the century were men. Did women let that stop them? Certainly not the women in the following chapters! They hiked up their skirts and scoffed at public disapproval with their incredible acts that were enough to scare the pants off most men.

Today, women participate in every kind of sport, from football to race-car driving, but imagine one hundred years ago, when women didn't have conveniences like electric hair curlers, microwaves, or cell phones. Back then, hand-held devices were sewing needles, butter churns, and washboards. Doing anything other than staying at home and taking care of husband and children was unthinkable. Women's clothing was neck-high and ankle-long with bunches of petticoats underneath. The trousers or skimpy costumes these female performers wore made their stunts all the more shocking, riveting, and fascinating.

From 1880 to 1929, these women, ranging in age from fifteen to sixty-three, demonstrated spunk, courage, derring-do, and nerves of steel equal to any male thrill-seeker. In the water, in the air, and in the circus, their extraordinary exploits, as awesome today as then, put their names in lights and their "feats" in headlines. They dove, drove, sped, and fed the public's appetite for spine-tingling, breath-holding entertainment. Besides, as Laurel Thatcher Ulrich said, "Well-behaved women rarely make history."

ZAZEL

Human Cannonball in Pink Tights

HAVE YOU EVER "CANNONBALLED" into a swimming pool? It's guaranteed to make a big splash as the diver smacks the water with a loud splat. The only danger is to people lounging poolside who may get drenched. Far more dangerous is the one performed in the circus—now *that's* a cannonball! A person being shot out of a cannon always hits the mark as a thrilling act.

The stunt dates back to the 1870s. You would assume that because of the times, only strong, tough men would perform this death defying feat. Surprise! It was a young girl who first claimed the fame, which made the act even more astonishing. The famous circus maestro P. T. Barnum had heard about Zazel's performances in Europe for years, and in 1880 he convinced her to come to America, where she became an immediate sensation.

Born Rosa Richter in London, England, in 1862, she made her first public appearance at age four. Her father, a well-known circus and dramatic agent, had her stand in for a sick child who was playing the part of Cinderella's sister in a juvenile pantomime at a famous theater. Rosa was an immediate favorite. Ballet and gymnastic training followed, and at twelve Rosa joined a Japanese troupe, learning balancing skills as they

traveled through Europe. A few years later, she began her cannon act and Zazel was "born."

Wearing pink tights, she curtsied to the crowd as she climbed into the mouth of the wooden cannon and rested her feet on a tiny platform inside, beneath which were strong springs. Her partner set off a deafening charge of gunpowder at the same instant that he released the springs, and Zazel was shot out of the cannon, flying with violent velocity through the air for a distance of over seventy-five feet before falling into a net. Her "splash" was met with thunderous applause.

Zazel became so famous that other women cannonballers who followed her "borrowed" her name because it held such fascination.

As an example of how scandalous it was for a woman to do this stunt in those early times, a forerunner of Zazel's human cannonball was another performer known as "Lulu." The real story is that Lulu was a man dressed as a woman, because it was believed that a woman doing something so dangerous would elicit more terror from the audience—and it probably did.

ANNIE EDSON TAYLOR

Queen of the Mist

ANNIE TAYLOR MADE A DIFFERENT SPLASH—in a treacherous waterfall! She celebrated her forty-third birthday on October 24, 1901, by going over Niagara Falls in a wooden barrel. Why would a widowed school-teacher from Michigan decide to try such a stunt at her age?

Because, simply put, she needed money.

About the only employment opportunity for women in those days was teaching school. Without a husband, or children, and almost penniless, Annie wanted something more than a measly teacher's salary to face what looked like struggling years ahead. She was convinced that her trip over the Falls would bring her fortune as well as fame.

On the big day, Annie approached the Falls in a long dress and fluttering hat. Prudish by nature, she made her male assistants turn their backs while she quickly changed into a short skirt (just below the knees) and then climbed inside her airtight wooden barrel. Thousands of people crowded the riverbanks to see with their own eyes this foolhardy woman try such a crazy (and illegal) stunt. Whether they were there to cheer her on or witness a disaster, they gave her the attention she wanted. *"Au revoir,"* she told them majestically. "I'll not say good-bye, because I'm coming back."

Custom-built, the barrel was four and a half feet high and four feet across, an extremely tight fit for any size adult. Annie scrunched herself inside, slipped her arms through a pair of leather shoulder straps—like a harness. Cushions were tucked around her and above her head, and she ordered the barrel to be bolted shut.

By strange coincidence, the empty barrel weighed 160 pounds, Annie herself weighed 160 pounds, and the Falls are 160 feet high. Seven iron hoops bound the barrel together, and the words QUEEN OF THE MIST were painted on its side. A hundred-pound anvil was tied to the bottom to keep the barrel upright when it floated. With Annie strapped inside,

a rowboat towed the barrel out to a place in the river where the water currents would carry her to the thundering Horseshoe Falls.

As a strong current picked up the barrel, the crowd fell silent. The barrel bobbed and flipped, and then splashed over the steep edge of the churning water. Despite the pillows, Annie's head banged violently against the sides of the barrel, but as cramped as she was, the only thing she could do was use her strong muscles to brace herself. Luckily, the barrel hit bottom upright. When rivermen opened the barrel, they yelled, "She's alive!" They fished her out, soaking wet, bruised and battered, but otherwise unharmed. It wasn't until later that she admitted she couldn't swim!

It had taken only seventeen minutes for Annie Taylor to accomplish what no one had ever done before: go over Niagara Falls in a barrel and live to tell about it. Her daring and determination brought her the flash of fame she so desperately wanted, but it was short-lived. Sadly, she died in poverty. Maybe if she had told reporters her real age when she performed the stunt, her fame might have lingered. Annie Taylor was twenty years older than what she claimed: she was sixty-three, not forty-three.

Since Annie's plunge, thirteen other people have attempted to go over the Falls in a barrel or similar contraption: three died and ten survived, including the only other woman who dared to risk her life.

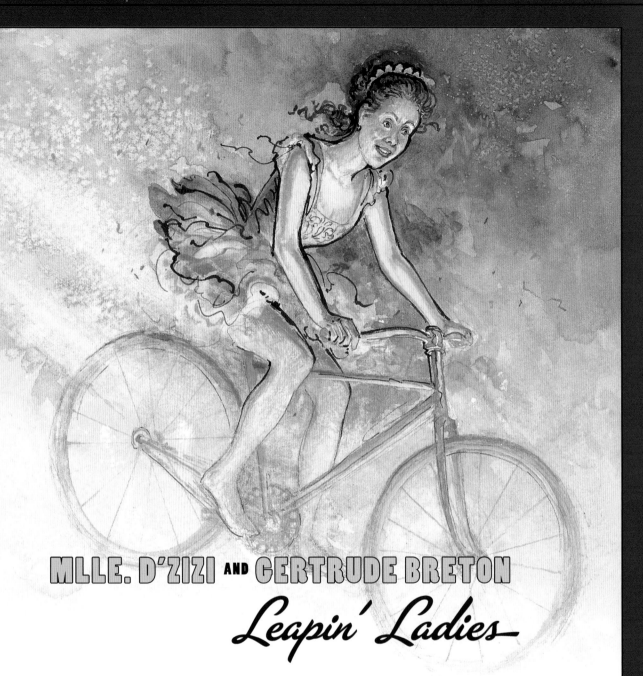

MLLE. D'ZIZI AND GERTRUDE BRETON
Leapin' Ladies

TWO WOMEN WHO LITERALLY LEAPED into fame were Mlle. d'Zizi and Gertrude Breton. Each one performed a fast-as-lightning bicycle act by rapidly riding down a steep incline and launching herself across a wide distance. Mlle. d'Zizi was billed as "The Dare Devil Ride Above a Yawning

Death Arch!" and Breton as "The Premier Leap-the-Gap Bicyclist of the World!"

French-born Mlle. d'Zizi thrilled American crowds in 1899 with her bicycle loop-the-loop act in the Walter Main Circus. At a terrific clip, she rode a bicycle down a long and steeply inclined ramp that turned up at the bottom, like an upside-down candy cane. She sailed up and out across a fifty-five-foot gap in which six elephants stood side by side, and landed safely on the ramp on the other side.

Bicycle acts were popular mainstays of all circus shows at the time. Audiences cheered basketball games played on unicycles and trick riders who jumped and somersaulted much like competitive skateboarders today. These acts were always performed under the Big Top.

What made Mlle. d'Zizi's stunt different was that it took place outside—and it was free and open to the public. Posters hyped and enticed audiences: "You can witness this superhuman triumph over nature without paying one cent of admission!" The act also helped sell bicycles, which had only recently been invented.

Like the question about the human cannonball Zazel's true identity, an allegation was made many years after d'Zizi's performances that "she" was actually a man dressed as a woman; evidently some circus fans noticed "she" had big feet. All the better to pedal with?

Gertrude Breton's perilous launch into air was less flashy and without elephants, but nevertheless exciting. Her act was a direct hurtle; she

dashed at a terrific rate of speed down a steep incline that extended from the roof of the hall, reaching the upward curved bottom that sent her sailing midair across a thirty-foot gap to a landing platform. The actual event took four seconds, far shorter than the amount of time the ecstatic audience's applause lasted.

She toured the country from 1905 to 1908, with the concluding performance at the Hippodrome in Convention Hall in Washington, D.C. A postcard with photos of her in her black bloomers and white shirtwaist promoted this early female Evel Knievel who did her hazardous vault without any protective gear or other safeguards.

In an interview with a reporter from *The Washington Post*, Breton acknowledged the risks. "Yes, there really is danger. The men who are doing this act have met with several serious mishaps, and one fatality has occurred. I have had some accidents myself. One was in Kansas City last year. I would not have been hurt but for the fact that a policeman who tried to catch me inadvertently struck my head with his club."

At the time, Breton was supposedly the only woman performing this daring act, and she always headlined the shows. Evidently there was no question about her femininity, because when she wasn't dressed in her riding costume, she looked like a demure college girl.

ISABELLE BUTLER AND THE
LA RAGUE SISTERS

Loopy Women Drivers

I F TWO WOMEN COULD DEFY GRAVITY riding
bicycles, why not three—in automobiles that looped
the loop? Perhaps these aerial auto somersaulters were as
"loopy" as the stunts they executed.

Isabelle Butler performed her spectacular "Dip of

Death," a one-car roller coaster with a twist, for the Barnum & Bailey Circus from 1905 to 1907. Dressed in a beautiful red gown, she was pulled up to an elevated platform in a chair and strapped into the seat of a primitive car. On her signal, the car dashed down the steep incline of the runway with the speed of an express train. When it reached the curve, the car turned upside down and shot into space across a forty-foot chasm. It landed right side up on another ramp and then looped a loop before finishing the run. Looking calm and poised, Isabelle would spring smiling from the car and wave both hands, to the thunderous applause of the audience.

Considered one of the most daring acts ever performed, the Dip of Death was so hazardous that no accident insurance company would risk a policy on her life. With good grounds, since the reason Isabelle took over the sensational feat was that the woman who originated it was killed in a fall resulting from a defective machine. For risking her life twice a day, Isabelle was paid $100 a second. (The stunt lasted only four seconds.)

Cars had only been recently invented and were a fascination all by themselves. The spectacle of a young attractive woman weighing eighty-two pounds, jeopardizing her life in an unpredictable machine weighing 1,800 pounds, was a real crowd thriller.

When asked if she was afraid the first time she attempted the stunt, Isabelle answered, "Frankly, I gave no thought whatever to the

danger of the act. I knew what had been done by one woman could be accomplished by another—if she had nerve enough." She added, "It's safer than Fifth Avenue!"

The Barnum & Bailey Circus owners were always on the lookout for new acts to prevent audiences from becoming bored. So they expanded the dangerous, one-car somersault act to two for the 1908 season. Two young women, Caroline and Nettie La Rague, drove separate cars, one following the other down a ninety-foot runway with a steep incline. The first car, painted red, dashed down the ramp, striking the half-loop at the bottom at a sharp angle, which catapulted the car into space, where it turned a full somersault in midair across a twenty-foot gap. The other car, painted blue, followed closely, but soared up and over the gap and underneath the red car as it completed revolving in the air. It landed on the opposite ramp just one second ahead of the red car. Whew!

Careful calculations determined that if the second car started just three-tenths of a second behind the first, the red automobile had just enough time to complete the somersault. The intricate engineering built into the equipment was so delicate that the weight of each sister had to be checked before each performance.

In spite of the popularity of "loop acts," 1909 was the last year "The Greatest Show on Earth" used an auto thrill act, because they were too dangerous. The La Rague sisters had become famous, not for spaghetti sauce, but for making audiences hold their breath in delight.

MAY WIRTH

World's Greatest Bareback Rider

MAY WIRTH ALSO PERFORMED SOMERSAULTS—
but hers were from one galloping horse to
another! She was just a teenager when she first headlined
for the Barnum & Bailey Circus in 1912 at Madison Square
Garden in New York City. The dainty and demure sixteen-

year-old was billed as "The Greatest Bareback Rider Who Ever Lived."

You might think that the acrobatics of a bareback rider were not nearly as dangerous as a human cannonball or a stunt-car driver, but May Wirth wasn't your ordinary circus equestrian.

Born in Australia, May came from a family of circus performers. She joined their act at age five, and by age thirteen she was already a star. A circus scout lured her to the United States, where her dainty size, sweet nature, and little-girl-styled hair tied with a big bow of pink ribbon made her an instant favorite. That pink bow became her trademark.

All of her tricks were thrilling, like her flawless forward somersault from a kneeling position, but her greatest trick was the backward somersault. Standing on the back of a galloping horse with her back to the horse's head, she did a complete somersault with a twist so that she landed on the horse facing forward. May was the first person to perform this backward somersault. Evidently, however, that wasn't challenging or risky enough for her, so she perfected a double backward somersault from one horse to a second horse galloping behind it, even while blindfolded!

After several years of performing her somersaults and handsprings so well that they were declared perfect, May added a trick that no one ever repeated. She was a master at vaulting, and to dramatize how sure-footed she was, she fastened two wicker market baskets over her feet. Then she leaped gracefully onto the back of a running horse. The stunt was a showstopper.

May claimed that she could ride anything on four feet. An attorney for another circus, who was probably hoping to discredit her, took her up on the challenge and dared her to ride his prize bull bareback. The untamed bull, named King Jess, had a mean disposition, and weighed 2,400 pounds. Undaunted by its size, not only did May ride the bull bareback, she rode him standing on her hands on his back. You wonder if she said, "I win. I'll ride your bull any day, 'Jess' for fun!"

As her name implied, May was "worth more than the price of a ticket." For twenty-six years she was the star performer in the center ring, often accomplishing thirty tricks in nine minutes, and thrilling audiences that sometimes included royalty and presidents. "I enjoy every minute of my act, particularly when I know there is someone in the crowd who appreciates riding," May said. "President [Woodrow] Wilson, before whom I have performed several times, is one of the best spectators I know." She was a favorite of Wilson's, and he came to watch May even after a stroke confined him to a wheelchair.

GEORGIA "TINY" BROADWICK
The Doll Girl of Aviation

EVEN MORE PETITE THAN MAY WIRTH, Georgia Broadwick, nicknamed "Tiny," made huge leaps in the air. The fifteen-year-old teenager, weighing less than ninety pounds and standing only 4' 6" tall, challenged aviation history by performing the first parachute jump—from a trapeze that was swinging below a hot-air balloon. Pretty scary even for today, but it was done in 1908—by a girl! When Georgia Broadwick did her daring stunt, young women were proper, demure, genteel, and definitely did not risk their necks with such crazy tomfoolery.

Her nickname of "Tiny" fit her to a T. She was so small she looked like a child, which was the reason she was billed "The Doll Girl of Aviation" when she performed. She dressed the part as well, wearing a baby cap with a chinstrap to keep her long blond curls from tangling in the ropes. She wore a white linen dress and demure, white-ruffled bloomers that polished off the image. Though her size was small, her spunk was enormous. Five years later, over Los Angeles, California, in 1913, she went on to become the first woman to parachute from an airplane.

One year later, she followed with another first by making the first free fall in history, tumbling through space before manually releasing the rip cord on her chute and landing in Lake Michigan. She even jumped over Niagara Falls from a hydroplane. And she always jumped headfirst.

You might wonder why a young woman's parents would allow her to do such dangerous acts. The answer is simple: Tiny inherited her

passion from her father, who was a parachute jumper before she was born, as was his father before him. So ballooning, parachuting, and jumping were all in the family, and Tiny's feet fit perfectly in their footsteps.

When she was nineteen years old, Tiny made her most important jump: she tested an aerial life preserver that her father had invented. The Chief of the Aviation Bureau of the U.S. Army and other military dignitaries watched as Tiny climbed into a military plane with the life preserver in a knapsack on her back. When the plane reached 1,400 feet at seventy-five miles per hour, Tiny dove headfirst toward the ground. Those watching held their breath—would the parachute open? Two seconds later, it did, and like a graceful bird, Tiny landed, laughing and saying it was easier than leaping from a balloon.

When a brigadier general commented, "You're plucky!" Tiny retorted, "Ha! I don't call it pluck. I call it joy. There's no real fun except far up in the air."

Her "fun" was a windfall for launching safety and skills in parachuting. Though she made over 1,000 jumps, she didn't make much money from them. She claimed, "I got all the Coca-Cola and sandwich money I needed and I was kid enough to enjoy it." Which she did until World War I began, when the "tiny" pioneer jumper retired, leaving a big mark in the pages of aviation.

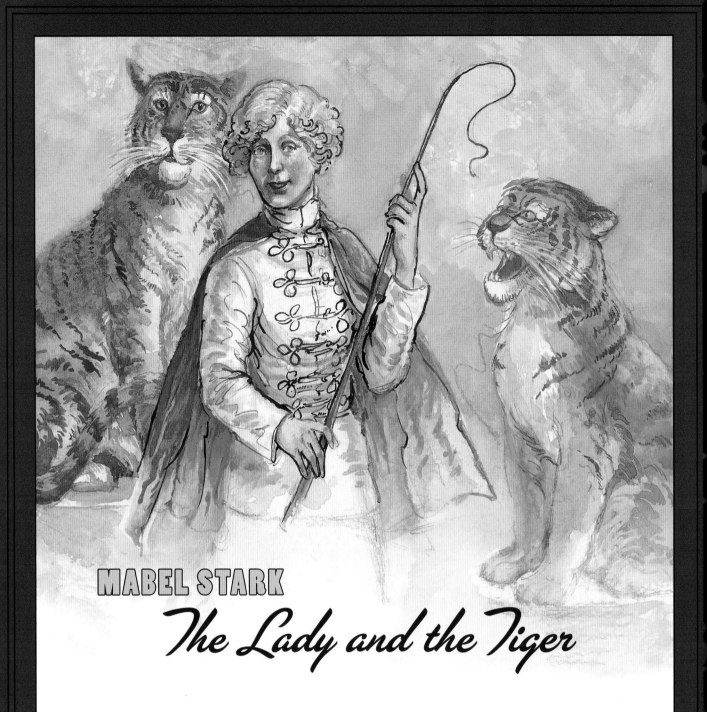

MABEL STARK
The Lady and the Tiger

MABEL STARK ALSO SCORNED DANGER—with a perilous animal act. The catchy refrain, "Hold that tiger! Hold that tiger!" from a popular song that came out in 1917 is the perfect description of her life as the world's greatest tiger tamer and trainer.

In the 1910s, when most girls dreamed of growing up to be wives and mothers, Mabel had an unusual desire to be a wild animal trainer. While other girls went on dates, she went to the zoo. Her fascination with "big cats" became an obsession that turned into a fifty-four-year-long career as "Marvelous Mabel Stark." During those performing years, she trained over 150 tigers.

Back then, job openings for animal trainers were few and far between, but for women—nonexistent! So Mabel's first training was as a nurse. She graduated from a Lexington, Kentucky, hospital, but in a very short time she hung up her uniform and cap. Like kids in early adventure stories, she ran off and joined a circus in California and took up animal training. Why? Because everyone told her it couldn't be done!

Standing five feet tall, weighing 100 pounds, with blond hair and sparkling blue eyes, Mabel proved that despite her size, she could crack the whip better than anyone else. Her bravado under the Big Top soon made her the biggest attraction for the Ringling Bros. and Barnum & Bailey Circus. Wearing her signature outfit, a skintight, white leather jumpsuit with thigh-high boots, she performed with twelve tigers—her "babies," as she called them—firmly but affectionately marching them through their paces.

Her favorite tiger was Rajah, having raised him from a cub, bottle-feeding him and even letting him sleep in bed with her. She trained him to do a wrestling act with her that left the audience gasping in fear, because it looked like she was being mauled.

One tiger that Mabel trained was so tame he became the circus mascot and posed for photos. She even taught Sammy to ride a bicycle. He also loved to ride in an automobile with his head out the window, which stopped traffic.

But these big "pussy cats" were not always gentle. She had more scars than a tiger has stripes. "There is no part of my body that doesn't bear the scars of tiger teeth and claws. I have been clawed seventy-five or eighty times. Six times I was given up for dead and told I'd never train again." Patched up after each narrow escape, she would return to the tiger cage wearing a cast or  walking with the aid of a cane. She claimed, "A tiger can whip anything but a gun, and me."

Her worst accident happened in 1926 in Bangor, Maine, and was almost fatal. The circus had been delayed by rains and pulled into the lot late with no time to feed the tigers before the performance. Wet and hungry, two aggressive tigers, Sheik and Zoo, expressed their discontent by attacking Mabel. She had to be carried out of the ring on a stretcher. It was a miracle she survived; the gashes and wounds took 378 stitches, and she was in and out of hospitals for the next two years.

Mabel's private life was as challenging and brazen as her tiger shows. Orphaned at age thirteen, she looked for love, but fared better with tigers than men. She married five times, ate a hamburger with her favorite beer for lunch every day, and lied about her age. She died in 1968 of a heart attack, according to the show-business newspaper *Variety*, which listed her age as seventy-nine.

GLADYS ROY AND GLADYS INGLE
Winsome Wing Walkers

MAGINE WALKING ON THE TOP WINGS of an airplane that looked like a giant dragonfly in flight! Two women named Gladys did exactly that. They were spellbinding examples of thrill-seekers in the 1920s called "barnstormers." The expression had nothing to do with weather but described traveling theater troupes that often performed in barns. When daring aviators began performing dangerous aerobatics in flying exhibitions, the title fit them as well. Who knows, some showoff pilot may have actually flown through a barn, christening the Barnstorming Era.

The 1920s opened up the skies to women: the Nineteenth Amendment to the Constitution was passed, giving women the right to vote. Newly empowered, they expressed their independence by wearing scandalously short dresses (above the knees!) and makeup, "bobbing" their hair, dancing in nightclubs and marathons, smoking and drinking, and pursuing jobs that had previously been men's turf only. To many, the behavior of these "flappers" was shocking.

That didn't stop the two wild and crazy Gladyses. With a vote in one hand and a paycheck in the other, they joined a handful of barnstorming women who grabbed the chance to explore the wild blue yonder and prove they belonged up in the air as much as men. Flying in the face of disapproval, they signed on with flying exhibition teams, thrilling crowds with their courageous acrobatics and death-defying stunts atop biplanes. What kept these flimsy contraptions airborne were two long wings, one lower and one upper, covered with fabric. The performers used these wings as their stage while the plane looped and spiraled in the sky. Much to the excitement of those watching from the ground, Gladys Roy and Gladys Ingle added their own sparkle and spin to wing walking.

Though they knew each other, they didn't perform together, as

each woman had her own specialty. Gladys Roy's was a famous dance that became popular during the Roaring Twenties. Strapped to the aircraft by a safety line on one leg, she threw up her arms with glee and danced the fast stepping Charleston on the wing of a plane as it raced through the clouds.

She also set records for her parachute jumps, even from an altitude as low as 200 feet. Photographers loved to snap pretty Gladys as she landed daintily from a jump and reached for her makeup. She often performed blindfolded and amused audiences with a rousing routine in which she and a male partner played an imaginary game of tennis from wing tip to wing tip on an airplane in flight.

Gladys Ingle had her own quiver of tricks. She was famous for shooting arrows at a target set up on one wing while she stood on the opposite wing of a flying biplane. Another demonstration of her marksmanship was an act like Annie Oakley's. She stood on one wing tip with her back to the target at the other end; holding a mirror in one hand and a rifle backward on her shoulder in the other, she fired several shots. Three out of four usually hit the target!

Her most dangerous stunt was the result of a wager—that she couldn't change an airplane wheel in flight. Ingle didn't hesitate to take the dare. With the replacement wheel strapped to her back, she transferred from one plane to another in midair, worked her way beneath the plane, maneuvered into a dangerous position to adjust the wheel axle that had slipped, slid the new wheel into place, and made her way back to the passenger cockpit. The pilot landed the plane safely, and she won the bet.

MABEL CODY

Just Plane Stunts

MABEL CODY WAS ANOTHER FEMALE DAREDEVIL in the air; she was an accomplished stuntwoman who not only performed her own aerial stunts but also applied her balancing skills to running her own flying circus— unheard of for a woman back then. Her business stationery advertised: wing walking; auto-to-plane transfers—with and without the use of ladders; parachute drops; and standing on top of a plane while it did a loop-the-loop. Her fearless acts were a huge hit with the public.

Daytona Beach on the east coast of Florida was a popular site for barnstorming and flying circuses in the 1920s. The beach was one long straightaway, making it ideal for car-to-plane transfers. Barely twenty years old, Mabel herself wasn't a pilot, but her acrobatic tricks and nerves of steel amazed the men in the cockpit, as well as the crowds on the ground. And she was going to raise the risk factor with an even more dangerous maneuver. In 1926, she transferred from a speedboat racing at full throttle to a rope ladder dangling from an airplane flying overhead. She was the first woman to perform the stunt—without a hitch.

The trick was all the more daring because Mabel had previously attempted the very same act and barely survived when the plane crashed and the boat caught fire. Another favorite stunt of hers was standing in the backseat of a car traveling seventy miles per hour down the beach as she grabbed the ladder of a plane roaring a few feet above her head. Even more precarious was the same leap from a motorcycle to a plane. The possibilities of mishaps didn't seem to faze her, despite the fact that she suffered several accidents, including missing a transfer and falling from an altitude of fifty feet.

Not everyone was thrilled with Mabel's daring deeds. A number of women in the area were indignant over her attire of pants, boots, and goggles. Alarmed by what they considered to be improper risk taking, they lit up her hotel's switchboard with protest calls. Mabel fumed to

the press, "Just because I happen to be a woman, a lot of women think it's their duty to remind me of the fact!"

Mabel knew that ballyhoo brought spectators, and no one was better at creating it than her husband, Curly, a well-known promoter of flying acts and a natural barker. He hyped the excitement as she performed delayed parachute jumps, danced on the wings of a plane while in the air, and stood erect on the top wing while the airplane performed a loop (wires ran up her pant leg to keep her from falling off).

Maybe it was Curly's flair for exaggeration that was responsible for their claim that Mabel was the niece of Buffalo Bill Cody, the Wild West showman. Almost every historical reference to Mabel states positively that she was definitely the niece of the famous man, except for one—the International Cody Family Association, which strongly denies it. Great publicity or the truth? Either way, there was no doubt that Mabel Cody and her flying circus were stars in the sky.

SONORA WEBSTER CARVER

The Girl on the High-Diving Horse

WHILE ANNIE TAYLOR CHOSE to challenge a huge body of water, Sonora Carver chose to dive into something much smaller: a tank of water about the size of a home swimming pool—on a horse!

Atlantic City, New Jersey, was the Disneyland of its day

in the early 1900s, and the Steel Pier was the greatest attraction. Called the playground of America, the Pier featured extraordinary live performances. But by far, the most popular, memorable, and mesmerizing act was the diving horse.

A diving tower with a platform stood sixty feet above a tank of water that was twenty feet wide and eleven feet deep. With a drumroll and a cymbal crash, the horse trotted up a ramp to the top of the platform, where a young female rider would spring onto its back, take hold of a leather strap around the horse, and urge it to jump. As the crowd held its breath, the horse and rider leaped into the air, then dove in, making an enormous splash that sent sheets of water over the sides of the tank, leaving it just half full. And the audience, many of them wet with spray, went wild.

Other young women performed dives on horses at the Steel Pier, but it was Sonora who stole the show every time with her bravado and charm. What led her to this strange but thrilling occupation? From the time she was five, Sonora loved horses—she once even tried to trade her brother for one! The first step up the ladder of her career began with a newspaper ad that her mother saw: "Wanted: Attractive young woman who can swim and dive. Likes horses, desires to travel."

In 1923, Sonora sat in the grandstand in Jacksonville, Florida, the troupe's winter quarters, fascinated by the horse-diving act, and with no idea that within the year she would be performing it. One year later,

earning fifty dollars a week, she made a splash in history when she plummeted forty feet on horseback into a tank of water.

For the seven years that Sonora was the star performer, she rode five horses. Like humans, horses have personalities: Klatawah was temperamental; Judas couldn't be trusted; Snow would do anything for a carrot; Lightning had a winning personality; Red Lips was her favorite. He was always eager to perform and, unlike the other horses that dove into the water at an angle, Red Lips did a nosedive, keeping his whole body vertical.

Sonora was riding Red Lips when a horrible accident occurred in 1931. When Red Lips jumped, his usual nosedive was off-kilter, and both horse and rider hit the water off-balance. Sonora struck the water flat on her face with her eyes open and immediately felt a stinging sensation. The impact of the bad dive resulted in detached retinas in both her eyes, blinding her at age twenty-seven.

What was truly amazing was that in spite of her handicap, Sonora continued to ride the high-diving horses blind for eleven years. The audiences never guessed that the woman making the daring dive couldn't see.

Sonora's autobiography, *A Girl and Five Brave Horses*, was the inspiration for the 1991 Disney film *Wild Hearts Can't Be Broken*. Both titles characterized her life. Sonora Carver lived to be ninety-nine years old. She died in 2003, a model of courage, fearlessness, and fervor for performing. She and her beloved horses made a big splash in history.

1809 MARY KIES was the first American woman to be awarded a U.S. patent, which was for a weaving technique.

1837 Oberlin College in Ohio was the first college in the United States to admit women.

1848 The first women's rights convention was held in Seneca Falls, New York.

1849 ELIZABETH BLACKWELL became America's first woman medical doctor.

1869 ESTHER MORRIS succeeds in making Wyoming the first territory to allow women to vote.

1869 SUSAN B. ANTHONY and ELIZABETH CADY STANTON cofounded the National Woman Suffrage Association.

1871 FRANCES WILLARD became the first female college dean at Evanston College for Ladies in Illinois.

1872 CHARLOTTE RAY graduated from Howard University and became the first African-American woman lawyer in the United States.

1879 BELVA LOCKWOOD was the first female lawyer allowed to practice before the U.S. Supreme Court.

1880 ZAZEL became the world's first human cannonball in the Barnum & Bailey Circus.

1885 Crack shot ANNIE OAKLEY was the most popular act in Buffalo Bill's Wild West show.

1889–1890 NELLIE BLY completed a trip around the world by boat and train in fewer than eighty days, setting a record and becoming the world's most famous female journalist.

1898 GENEVRA MUDGE was the first woman to drive a car in America; it was an electric car.

1899 MLLE. D'ZIZI thrilled circus crowds by riding a bicycle across a fifty-five-foot gap and over six elephants.

1901 ANNIE EDSON TAYLOR was the first person to go over Niagara Falls in a barrel and survive.

1905 The first woman millionaire was SARAH BREEDLOVE, known as Madame C. J. Walker, who created a line of cosmetics for African Americans.

1905–1907 ISABELLE BUTLER performed her spectacular "Dip of Death," a one-car roller coaster ride.

1905–1908 GERTRUDE BRETON performed her daring bicycle leap.

1908 SISTERS LA RAGUE performed an aerial auto race.

1908 ANNIE SMITH PECK was the first mountaineer, man or woman, to climb the highest peak in Peru, a height of 21,812 feet, at age sixty.

1910 BLANCHE STUART SCOTT became the first woman pilot in America.

1911 HARRIET QUIMBY became the first woman to solo a plane across the English Channel.

1911 MARIE CURIE won the Nobel Prize in chemistry, for discovering a new source called radium.

1912–1938 MAY WIRTH, "The Greatest Bareback Rider Who Ever Lived," was a master at vaulting onto a horse and at doing double somersaults from one horse to another.

1913 GEORGIA "TINY" BROADWICK made the first parachute jump from an airplane.

1916 JEANNETTE RANKIN became the first woman elected to the House of Representatives.

1920 The Nineteenth Amendment to the U.S. Constitution is finally passed, giving women the right to vote.

1920s GLADYS ROY and GLADYS INGLE became famous as wing walkers.

1920s MABEL STARK was the greatest tiger tamer in history.

1924 SONORA WEBSTER CARVER was the most popular of the women who rode the high-diving horses at Atlantic City.

1925 NETTIE TAYLOR ROSS became the first woman to serve as governor of a state, which was Wyoming.

1926 MABEL CODY became the first woman to successfully transfer from a speeding boat to a rope ladder dangling from a flying airplane.

1926 GERTRUDE EDERLE was the first woman to swim the English Channel.

1931 JANE ADDAMS was the first American woman to win the Nobel Peace Prize.

1932 HATTIE WYATT CARAWAY of Arkansas was the first woman elected to the U.S. Senate.

1932 AMELIA EARHART completed the first nonstop transatlantic flight by a woman.

1933 FRANCES PERKINS was named by President Franklin Delano Roosevelt as his Secretary of Labor, becoming the first woman cabinet member.

SOURCES AND ACKNOWLEDGMENTS

Researching the lives of people who lived decades or even a century ago is just like a jigsaw puzzle, finding pieces that fit into a whole picture. In a way, that's how this book came about.

It was while I was doing research for a book about a male daredevil who jumped Niagara Falls in the 1880s, that I "found" Annie Edson Taylor. The next piece of the puzzle appeared at the San Diego Aerospace Museum, where I was tracking down stories about early women pilots and discovered Georgia "Tiny" Broadwick. Hmm, I wondered, were there other women who lived at the turn of the century that performed life-risking stunts? My idea had begun to sprout.

Of the fourteen women in the book, I found the least amount of information on Gertrude Breton. The key clue was a postcard with two addresses, but contacts with historical societies in Kansas and Oregon produced nothing, and she wasn't mentioned in any books on the history of bicycling. Luckily, an e-mail question to the American Memory Fellows at the Library of Congress produced five brief newspaper articles describing her performances.

In contrast, there were copious amounts of information on two of the women. The archives in The New York Public Library for the Performing Arts contained a trove of newspaper and magazine articles and memorabilia of May Wirth and the Local History Department of the Niagara Falls Public Library had folder after folder of information about Annie Edson Taylor, including handwritten letters.

A number of libraries had books that provided historical "snapshots" of circus women and one listed circus museums. Thanks to Marcy Murray at the Circus Museum of The John and Mable Ringling Museum of Art in Sarasota, Florida; Erin Foley at the Circus World Museum Library in Baraboo, Wisconsin; Kristen Spangenberg at the Cincinnati Art Museum in Cincinnati, Ohio; and Mary Witkowski, head of the Historical Collections at the Bridgeport Public Library, Bridgeport, Connecticut, for their interest in the project and sharing their resources.

A special thanks to Merri Lindgren, librarian at the Cooperative Children's Book Center at the University of Wisconsin-Madison, who was my hands and eyes for delving into the riches at the Museum Library at Baraboo.

The early period proved to be the biggest challenge: in many cases the only resources were archival files, newspaper clippings (often so fragile the paper crumbled in your hand), and tidbits in out-of-print books. Internet sites offered fragments of information that were sometimes contradictory, confirming that it should not be considered as the sole source of information.

Only two women had books written about them: *Hold That Tiger,* by Mabel Stark with Gertrude Orr, published in 1938 by Caxton; and *A Girl and Five Brave Horses,* by Sonora Carver, as told to Elizabeth Land, published in 1961 by Doubleday.

Other titles that included profiles or references were: *Daredevils of Niagara,* by Andy O'Brien, published by Ryerson Press in 1964; *Barnstormers & Speed Kings,* by Paul O'Neil, published by Time-Life Books in 1981; *A Pictorial History of the American Circus,* by John and Alice Durant, published by A. S. Barnes and Co. in 1962, *Women of the Air,* by Judy Lomax, published by Dodd, Mead in 1987; *The Barnstormers: Flying Daredevils of the Roaring Twenties,* by Don Dwiggins, published by Grosset & Dunlap in 1968; *Heroes Without Legacy: American Airwomen, 1912-1944,* by Dean Jaros, published by University Press of Colorado in 1993.

Curiosity about the past can lead to amazing discoveries, and sometimes the search is as exciting as the discovery itself. I hope you'll find this picture of the lives and times of these daring women as fascinating as I do.